WORLD CELEBRATIONS

DIWALI

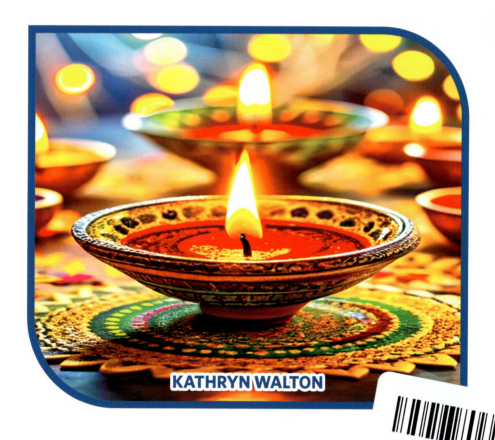

KATHRYN WALTON

PowerKids press

Published in 2026 by The Rosen Publishing Group, Inc.
2544 Clinton Street, Buffalo, NY 14224

Copyright © 2026 by The Rosen Publishing Group, Inc.

All rights reserved. No part of this book may be reproduced in any form without permission in writing from the publisher, except by a reviewer.

First Edition

Editor: Greg Roza
Book Design: Rachel Rising

Photo Credits: Cover, p. 1 Ashish01818/Shutterstock.com; pp. 4, 6, 8, 10, 12, 14, 16, 18, 20 Vjom/Shutterstock.com; p. 5 Raushan_films/Shutterstock.com; p. 7 AstroVed.com/Shutterstock.com; p. 9 Hugo Zavala/Shutterstock.com; p. 11 StockImageFactory.com/Shutterstock.com; p. 13 KACHALOV/Shutterstock.com; p. 15 rohit patel15797/Shutterstock.com; p. 17 Pikoso.kz/Shutterstock.com; p. 19 PhotoGullak/Shutterstock.com; p. 21 Mariusz S. Jurgielewicz/Shutterstock.com.

Some of the images in this book illustrate individuals who are models. The depictions do not imply actual situations or events.

Library of Congress Cataloging-in-Publication Data

Names: Walton, Kathryn, 1993- author.
Title: Diwali / Kathryn Walton.
Description: [Buffalo] : PowerKids Press, [2026] | Series: World celebrations | Includes index.
Identifiers: LCCN 2025012623 (print) | LCCN 2025012624 (ebook) | ISBN 9781499452105 (library binding) | ISBN 9781499452099 (paperback) | ISBN 9781499452112 (ebook)
Subjects: LCSH: Divali—Juvenile literature. | Fasts and feasts—India—Juvenile literature.
Classification: LCC BL1239.82.D58 W357 2026 (print) | LCC BL1239.82.D58 (ebook) | DDC 394.265/45-dc23/eng/20250402
LC record available at https://lccn.loc.gov/2025012623
LC ebook record available at https://lccn.loc.gov/2025012624

Manufactured in the United States of America

CPSIA Compliance Information: Batch #CSPK26. For Further Information contact Rosen Publishing at 1-800-237-9932.

CONTENTS

A Festival of Lights 4
Hindu Gods 6
Rows of Lights 8
Getting Ready for Diwali 10
At the Temple 12
Good Fortune. 14
Let's Eat! 16
Brothers and Sisters 18
Diwali Around the World 20
Glossary 22
For More Infomation 23
Index. 24

The Festival of Lights

Diwali is the Hindu **Festival** of Lights! It is a celebration of light winning over darkness. It lasts for five days. Diwali is celebrated in different ways depending on the country or place. Diwali has been celebrated for a long time in India, Indonesia, Malaysia, Nepal, and many other countries.

Hindu Gods

Hinduism is a very old religion that honors many gods. Diwali is a time to celebrate them. People celebrate the god Rama because he beat a **demon** named Ravana who had 10 heads! Some people celebrate the marriage of the goddess Lakshmi and the god Vishnu.

Rows of Lights

The word "Diwali" means "row of lights." Diwali celebrations include oil lamps called diyas. These lamps are placed around the home. They are placed in **temples** and on walls in public. Some people put them in tiny boats and let them float away!

Getting Ready for Diwali

Families prepare for Diwali by cleaning and **decorating** their homes. They put out diyas. They create colorful circles on floors and tabletops called rangolis. Rangolis are made with colorful powders, flowers, and grains of rice. These things are carefully placed to create colorful shapes.

At the Temple

During Diwali, Hindus go to temples. They pray to the gods and to their ancestors, or the people in their family that lived before them. Temples are also decorated with diyas and bright colors. People place flowers around pictures of the gods.

Good Fortune

The third day of Diwali is the main day of the festival. Families open their doors and windows. They put diyas and candles in their windows. They do this to welcome good **fortune** into their homes. At night, people enjoy watching **fireworks**!

Let's Eat!

The foods that people eat during Diwali are different depending on the country. One thing that is the same is the importance of honoring the family. Large family dinners are common. On the second day of Diwali, people like to visit friends and family and share sweet treats!

Brothers and Sisters

On the last day of Diwali, brothers and sisters celebrate each other. Girls make their brothers' favorite foods. Sometime they feed brothers by hand! Sisters paint a red mark on their brother's foreheads as a sign of love and **respect**. Brothers and sisters give each other gifts.

Diwali Around the World

Diwali has been celebrated in India and other countries for a long time. Today, there are Diwali celebrations all over the world. Festivals in the United States and Canada include prayer, food, music, dancing, and fireworks! The White House in Washington, D.C., has held a yearly Diwali celebration since 2003.

GLOSSARY

decorate: To make something interesting or beautiful by adding things to it.

demon: A bad spirit.

festival: A time of celebration in honor of something or someone special.

fireworks A display of explosions and light high in the air created by the burning of chemicals.

fortune: Good luck.

respect: Showing good manners and treating others kindly.

temple: A building where people pray and worship.

FOR MORE INFORMATION

BOOKS
Joshi, Anjali. *Why We Celebrate Diwali: Everything to Know About Your Favorite Holiday.* Oakland, CA: Callisto Publishing, 2025.

Kothari, Dev. *One Diwali Day.* Somerville, MA: Candlewick Press, 2025.

WEBSITES

Diwali: Festival of Lights
kids.nationalgeographic.com/pages/article/diwali
Read more about Diwali at National Geographic Kids.

Hindu Deities Facts for Kids
kids.kiddle.co/Hindu_deities
Learn about the many Hindu gods and goddesses at this detailed website.

Publisher's note to educators and parents: Our editors have carefully reviewed these websites to ensure that they are suitable for students. Many websites change frequently, however, and we cannot guarantee that a site's future contents will continue to meet our high standards of quality and educational value. Be advised that students should be closely supervised whenever they access the internet.

INDEX

A
ancestors, 12

B
brothers and sisters, 18

D
diyas, 8, 10, 12, 14

F
fireworks, 14, 20
foods, 16, 18, 20

G
gods, 6, 12

H
Hindu, 4, 6, 12

I
India, 4, 20

R
rangolis, 10

T
temples, 8, 12

W
White House, 20